tide tables
and tea with god

CASSONDRA WINDWALKER

tide tables
and tea with god

a story of suicide and sea changes

OTIS BOOKS
MFA WRITING PROGRAM
Otis College of Art and Design
LOS ANGELES ▰ 2021

Book design and typesetting: Alexi Gehring

ISBN-13: 978-9980-2-4307-2

OTIS BOOKS
MFA WRITING PROGRAM
Otis College of Art and Design
9045 Lincoln Boulevard
Los Angeles, CA 90045

https://www.otis.edu/mfa-writing/otis-books
otisbooks@otis.edu

My husband and I moved to Alaska in 2017. To make that happen, we took a sixty percent cut in income and gave up our home to live on the property of my husband's new job. These poems were all written during the following two years. A few weeks before the move, a dear friend died by suicide. A little over a year later, a cousin with whom my husband had grown up died by suicide as well. Meanwhile, my youngest child was involved in a horrific car accident that claimed the lives of two other people. My husband's only son was diagnosed with schizophrenia and died of an overdose a few months later. But there are more ways to die than merely stopping breathing. This book explores some of the ways we die and some of the ways we live despite incursions on body and mind. Both my husband and I are solitary people by nature, so while finding our way through this series of traumas, we spent much of our time outdoors and learned everything we could about the unique blend of cultures that make up the Alaskan population.

This book of poetry is dedicated to the jellyfish, strange, ineluctable travelers whose journeys so often end alone, stranded by the tide on a shore where they do not belong.

contents

the sea is a stranger

lift all boats

the shivering stilled, but still I lay
splayed on mud flats, fish eyes staring
at a sun who would not stare back:
skin shriveled and vision blanched,
I waited on the tide to lift my bones,
to make debris a coracle, my sighs a sail,
but high tide is not high enough today.

even a ship when stranded is only driftwood,
the sea becomes arroyo when it had been road,
and a star-empty sky only a map with no lines:
so if I cannot be traveler, let me be landmark,
tie my hair around these stones,
lay out my bones to leave a trail, and bury my words
     in the wind:

I lie splayed on mud flats, waiting for the tide.

beachcomber

my pockets are full:
bits of broken shell, wave-carved woods,
and wandering bones bite into my thigh,
reminding me that I too am a jumble

a pile of artifacts in someone else's pocket,
lost kisses, dropped intentions,
broken words that carry only inflection,
inflection, and no meaning:

what will be the sum of the day's finds
when the pockets are turned out?
will my misplaced pieces find rest
on a shelf like this mermaid's cigarette,
this whale's rebuff, or be discarded,
debris without a name?

I smile on my treasures,
line them up in the sun,
spin stories on their jagged rims
and promise to remember.

A Broken Curve

I found it too late, of course:
a perfect spiral flaring into infinity,
its fine, delicate walls carved out
by an ocean whose strength cannot be fathomed,
its colors, impossible in their singularity,
measured out in a pattern more precise
than the mortal mind can imitate

yet, though born of the wildest and fiercest
of wombs, though this tiny shell traveled
hundreds of miles, hundreds of tides,
and kept itself, itself, intact,
the paltry rocky shore on which I stand
proved more brutal than its form could bear –

this shell has lost its spiral. I cannot hear
the voice of the ocean in its curve,
I cannot find the math to make it whole.
even the strongest may break, break irreparably,
when dashed upon a boulder,
but there is beauty in the broken pieces yet.

day and night at the top of the world

even the ocean's teeth are chattering,
clattering icy froth over chunks of coal
and earth-burnt rocks – no warm sand here,
and the glancing gaze of the sun merely mocks,
a scythe of light that barely carves a curve
over the horizon, scarce illumination
and no heat, no heat:

here subterfuge is only weight,
bluster and bravado snatched away by the wind.
what the earth does not swallow,
the sea sweeps away, with no more malice
or regard than the man bears the ant:
there is a consolation in the severity of ice,
solace in a night that will have its way,
string its lights, play its music,
insistent on the company of stars in a world of screens.

heavy pockets

I strode in, and the tide fled.
never mind, I said,
pretending to look away,
pretending to wonder at lost sea stars
and tumbling spirals
but I was only filling my pockets
with rocks and sea glass and anger,
waiting for her to creep up to my ankles again –

again into the cold, into the deep,
into the dark, but rocks and sea glass
and anger belong to the sea, after all:
at her command, they rise
from the depths and float on the froth,
and when she casts them out,
they cannot return without her permit.

So here on the shore I stand,
I and the rocks and the glass and the rage.

small stories

the sea tells all her secrets
to the shell, but the shell tells none
to me: that susurrous whisper only lies,
tempting me, taunting me,
while silent in the spiral waits –
what? – I will ask the sand
that skitters in my palm
and believe all it says.

I Will Lie Here

some crave the violence and drama
of the tide at its crest, all whitecaps
and roaring, the exhilaration of near-drowning
that isn't near anything
so much as reluctant retreat

me, I wait for the ocean to turn its back,
wait on that sultry, over-the-shoulder glance
that lures me in, the promise of treasures
carefully curated, their stories told
in strange tongues, traced out with wet fingers
on bare sandy skin, sagas whose oracles
I can almost, almost see
there
shimmering just beneath the water,
whispering away from my feet,
before their murky lights blink out
in the glare of this ceaseless sun:

let others chase their tumults
on the ceiling of the sea: I will lie here
on its floor and watch light
become a lost wanderer,
I will fill my ears with currents
until my veins becomes trenches, my bones the cavern ribs.

Restive Sister

she suffers me, this sea.

accustomed to my rambles along her tide,
she measures the depth of my steps,
permits my insolent incursions

this time
one more time
one more time

but we both know I am alien here.
her air is poison to my lungs
and my words roll like shells in her hands,
shaped and changed but eventually
tossed out: even with all their edges worn away,
they do not fit in her inconstant space:

every syllable pretends at boundary
that she sweeps away.
she suffers me, this sea,
because in suffering we are familiar to each other,

but familiar does not make friends.

timing

I found the sea-star too late
but only just: salty tears still clung
to its beaded skirts, and though
its tiny tentacles seemed (almost) to move
if I stared at them long enough,
its form held a finality I could not persuade
to alter. still, I flung it back
to the waves, as if mother-sea could provoke
what stranger-me could not,
as if that wild familiar rhythm
could coax the star back to twinkling
in a sea-sky – forlornest of hopes.

I found you too late, too,
imagined hope where there was none,
mistook death-spasms for a life fight.
You are back in the sea now,
tumbling in a wild surf
and lost to us, but perhaps not lost at all.

black water, black sky

something is adrift

where black sky meets black water
where the sad meet the silent
something drifts, farther and farther out

the current is strong, and there is no will –
do not strain to hear a cry,
do not cast out a rope
what drifts, drifts silent and still

if you will pull the broken
from this sea, you must cast yourself
into the water, into the blackness, too,
you must drown your own eyes
in the night, succumb your own breath
to the waves, you must be fiercer
than the tow, you must bring hope

with you, for the drifter has none.

sea-glass

my step-sister does not own me,
rarely regards my footsteps on her threshold
and never does she seek me out,
but today I hear a keening in her tuneless song,
a thread of mourning that ties together
her and me and our common pater:

she has poured me a glass – rare concession –
and I drink her frothing, salty vintage
in silent salute to our griefs,
common and uncommon, shared and unshared:
I taste the forests she has uprooted,
the ships she has swallowed,
the storms she has birthed, the stories
whose tangled alphabets she daily spells
in lines upon the shore, though we are all illiterate,
and I cannot fault her for her distance.

What is my name beside her?
still, today, she shares this glass with me,
today she adds my paragraph to her unread book.

repentance at high tide

what angel wept beneath your waves last night,
Cliodhna, that morning brings such terrible remorse?

I am not used to seeing you penitent:
this sudden fierce pity of yours
leaves me only more fearful – I can hardly bear
to watch you rush upon the shore,
arms full of your brigand bounty, as you plead
with earth and sky to let you restore
what is irreparable, even for Manannan's daughter:

forests, rent of root and limb, froth in the tide,
hulls and decks and doorframes matchstick in the sand,
whole colonies of seaweed and strewn sponge corpses
only begin the tale of your penance,
and in the frantic lines of verse, writ large
in sand and foam, I read more stories
than my heart can hold – poor Cliodhna.
who has convicted you of your wickedness?

you and I are currents that cannot change course –
(will not, will not is truer) – thieves and devourers
who know only how to make delight of death.
tonight you will creep back and reclaim these treasures
you are so desperate to offer up this morn,
tonight this longing for absolution will surrender
itself to the moon, tonight we will swallow our sorrows.

pressed down, running over

she is graveyard and birthing stool,
repository of drowned hopes, bearer of bones,
colonizer of moons: I anoint my feet
with her oil, count the bodies
of her children laid out on the sand,
and wash my hair with her tears.

she mourns beautifully, savagely,
and without regret – a wholly inhuman grace.
we know only love with guilt,
bury our griefs under stones of remorse,
and force the dead to wear our penance
as a name – not so this sea,
first among mothers, first among mourners.

I will drink her sorrow
till it tastes like my own.

a chorus of broken limbs

no leaves left

these woods know the worth
of a quick good-bye: color does not linger long
on these grey limbs, and sentiment and sympathy
find no sustenance where lichen and moss and mold
delight to undo all the seams
summer had thought to sew:

pretty birds, pretty people, pretty words
have fled these parts,
and the cold, the bone, the stone, and the brine
that remain offer no apology, no refuge,
and seek no succor to sustain their forms.

early autumn rain

I am heavy, heavy,
like birch leaves, pregnant with rain,
filling up, spilling over,
life: on the verge of expectoration,
explosion, expulsion –

I have been filled
Let me empty
Let me labor, let me deliver
I am ripe no more.

One more dawn, one more frost,
I will be rotten.

Eat me now,
juices spilling from your lips
while they are sweet:
I would be food and not wine,
mother, not lover,
teacher, not seducer.
Eat me now, while I am still sweet.

castaways

how well they marry, this golden leaf
and this umber, set adrift from their disparate limbs
by time and privation, a liberty lent
that to the green leaf seems only an end
but grants these all this season's grace

to lie and lying, find consummate
in the shape and color of the other, a perfect peace:
here they breathe the loamy air
of the forest floor, here they listen,
fixed and transfixed, to shared whispers
no wind could ever have carried,
here divergent growth becomes singular end

for after all, this liberty is only lent.
debtors at the last to a mystery no root can resist,
no zephyr can outrun, all their colors will crumble
into dust, indistinguishable each from the other,
as yellow and brown fade into the stuff of stars,
and darkness draws them on into a new, undreamt season.

sit

It waits in me,
the letting-go, the releasing

I am become the stillness
of a breathless day, a day that needs
no wind, no gust to break

this last strand of leaf that clings
to tree, to then, to was, to warmth

together we are filled, broken clear
of our emptying, overflowing
with color that will feed none
but ourselves – I taste cold in every cell

and the leaf falls, I fall,
no longer worker but wanderer,
our only resolve to beauty, beauty, beauty.

spendthrift

the trees have spent nearly all
their currency, gold coins heaped on the floor
of the forest hall – I call them profligate,
but persuaded, I toss my own leatherbacks
into the drifting piles: printed on skin,
backed by time, my hoarded treasure buys
me this, only this, and it seems enough:

the sound of a leaf falling through still autumn air,
a black branch, a blue sky, a grey cloud, a yellow dress,
the flavor of your good-bye, strong in my mouth.

The Last Leaf

I am ready for a storm, said the last leaf,
brown and brittle and withered on a trembling stem:
she had persisted through the gales of autumn,
despising and finally discarding the agate colors
of her sisters, choosing rather to embrace the frost
in whose limbs she lost the last of her supple strength.

now earth is grey, her fallen sisters long lost
to sight beneath the sheeting ice and snow.

I am ready for a storm, said she, unwilling
to end mere litter on a snowy hill,
unwilling to cling any longer to a somnolent tree.

Shred me, tear me, fling me
on the gusts till I am dust, said the last leaf.
Let me dream at the end I am become the storm.

castle conquered

a marvel of cooperative construction,
the paper wasps' nest has hung in the alder
all summer, beautifully symmetrical
and seemingly unassailable, its armies sallying
out on regular patrol from the tiny entrance
with its tiny drawbridge: all season I watched –
from a safe distance, of course – entranced
by their singularity of purpose, the deliberate beauty
of their survival, the precision of their craft,
but today, summer and her strange drought
hustled out of sight, over the mountains
and across the sea, as autumn rushed in as a torrent:

it can only have fallen, surely,
weighted with the rain, shredded by wind,
but I find no race of it, not even
scraps of paper clinging to wet leaves.
I wonder where they went,
where I will go,
as the cold sweeps on and on and on.

as the smoke clears

blackened corpses stand their own headstones:
an innumerable army born of some cauldron,
the staring sockets where eyes and limbs
once rested, now macabre perches
for only the most exhausted of migrators,
who rest but a moment on the charred shafts
before the scent of all that ashy marrow
on the wind drives them on – the earth, too,
is scorched, unremitting black testament to the raging fury
that bent all its breath and power to consume
these mountains and meadows, but there is a glee
unmistakable in these wrecked and wretched
silhouettes, a triumph in the sooty faces:

life lies still fixed in the roots that churn
beneath the charcoal loam, a resurrection
waits only on the spring and her certain rains.
fire is a pretender, a masquerade of devastation,
but at the last she bends her energies
to create, to pound out with vicious fists
and cruel hammers a form the stone knew not to dream.

bell, book, and snowfall

whispers ping-pong on glassy tree trunks,
breathy huffs of air that promise
some secret hilarity shared among the winter pines,
old jokes and bits of dryad gossip the juicier
for their oh-so-quiet rush of banter
barely breathed out in this still and icy air:

let summer nymphs chatter and clatter
and dither at the top of their lungs,
let autumn's dancers stomp their feet
and clap their hands in mad jigs and reels.
winter is the season of secrets and confidences,
of mysteries and enigmas that lend weight
and solemnity even to the tiny chirpers
as they teeter-totter on snow branches,
that make map of the hare's rambling courses,
and imagine ritual and wisdom in the gaze of the moose.

madness is a constellation, broken

I Hang On The Turning

light-blind and starlorn, I am bowed
beneath the weight of this unrelenting sun,
borne down, pressed against the earth:

I will seek the darkness here,
search out some strands of night
that may have burrowed beneath the summer flowers
or that lie, more patient than I,
along the currents of the sea and wait
till the earth spills out this long, long day
and fills my cup again with that sweet cool elixir,
that somber respite that quiets my ache
and promises communion with my black heart:

I will pin up the shards of my bones
on the constellations, I will stretch
the paper of my skin as a lantern on the moon,
I will breathe and it will not hurt.

I Must Be Off

symmetry and straight lines:
this tendency to chaos is overstated
dropped stitches draw the eye
even madness tends to perseverate
on points of order – if this pattern
is no more than poor brief imposition,
then its persistence is unanticipated obstinacy:

whether stars or shell or this moribund mind,
even the unravelling, unwinding, disordering,
is orderly in all its wild undoing –
though my orbit grows elliptical,
and in time, in time, in regular time,
I must be off, my traverse will be well-mapped
by all the means and spirals [not] lost before me.

greyline mornings

dawn rises like a ghost,
drifting into the darkness
with little expectation of recognition:
even the sun droops to learn
his name has been forgotten,
these few brief hours reserved
for him claimed by fog and cloud:

aborted illumination haunts the edges
of things – the edge of a frozen blade
of grass, the edge of a falling leaf,
the edge of my words as they, too,
bide in shadow, rest in night,
dread the return of longer days and fiercer light.

cold hands, cold heart

the mouth of the sun settles hungrily
on the tops of the trees, licks alight
the bare limbs with the ardor of a lover
divided by a long, cold, black night,
but no answering desire rises like fog,
no blood-rush warms beneath the kiss:

bright and familiar, this fire brings no heat,
and the ice encapsulating each trembling twig
holds fast its own, undaunted by the threat
of another's caress, unmoved by summer's tired kisses.

I know I'm losing it

it is a fever, a fire, that travels
through my nerves, my veins, and torments
will into unwilling action – I would stop
this useless scribbling, cease this pretense
now, when the collapse of wants has met
the collapse of mind, and both are staggering,
impasse'd, upon the field –
but this fire forces the ink still to spill
and make mockery of all my means:

I will lose all – it comes apace –
but not so soon as to render me insensible
to the certainty of its advance.
Cruel ending, that must monologue so.

Gemma Passing

the stars tonight are shaken loose,
tumbling out of place – but no,
the stars look on, unaltered and unmoved
by this fiery show of burning ingles,
these lesser sparks who with abandon
blaze but a brief and single light:

it is only a goddess striding by
on regular patrol, the gauze of her train
caught up in our ragged welkin,
scattering sequins and diamonds as if
they were no more than cosmic dust,
hurtling madly across the courses of the universe.

the stars wink out

I'll admit I was distracted, distracted by the everything
            of silence,
an abyss and void of sound that swallowed
even the songs of the stars,
swallowed time and presence and thought
so that I could only senseless stand
in the court of the galaxies and lose myself
in the counting of names and the naming of numbers,
my eyes dazzled with distances and dreams
of light whose cold silver heat I felt
on my face, though their impetus was long cold
and dark and dead: one by one

and one again, I chased the fiery streaks,
the ancient travelers burning out an end
to journeys across our skies, and so
I was distracted, discovering too late
a new, more malefic darkness had arrived,
suffusing the skies and suffocating the stars
out of my sight: so creeps this madness,
a patient bloom upon the mind that steals
more lucidity day by day.

inchoate immortal

sky presses, presses, presses,
heaps clouds on my eyes
buries my limbs, my trunk, my head
under the weight of unseen stars,
fills my ears with the silence
of their absence, my cell and stem and stoma
with unness of what was known,
with darkness not dark at all
but only amorphous once-was-light

we have all unbecome
so I am better buried here
peering against vapor and mist
immobile beneath the entirety of nothing.
let me forget my name.
there remains no edge against which
it may echo.

hook, line, and sinker

it pounds against my skin,
bleating from my bones,
this fury crying out! out! out!
but there is no out,
until expiration – still the flesh thins
and the veins vibrate,
strung like catgut on the fiddle:
I am barely clinging to my carnal shape –
I trace its smoke on icy glass
and watch its vapor vanish in the dawn.
I do not want to hold my place,
my name is weariness to my ear,
my wanting all that I despise in me.
Best set a marker, bury a post,
tie a line – else a wind, a strong wind,
any wind, and I am gone.

the entropy of faith

that I shall need no comfort then
is hardly comfort to me now:
even cognizant of clear consciousness
I find nothing less than terror
in consideration of the void:
if stars do not sing, if trees do not listen,
if life is no more than sleight of hand,
an illusion of energy and matter,
if there is no now because there is no then,
then I would unravel it all,
but this, too, is futility –

we have imagined pattern
and order and laws as if what is
must be, but these too are only constructs,
insistences of a mind who wishes
to be more than merely a mass,
who longs to hear and to attend
to any voice beyond its own,
to find immortality even if
it is only named a law of motion.

winter incant

the night is silent, the night is still.

I am silent, and I am still.
under the stars, I am scrubbed out,
erased, the edges I had drawn
around my being fading into the darkness.

breath slows, beat picks up the rhythm
that rises, calm and incurious,
from the weight of the frozen earth,
pressing up against my feet,
and the farther awhen I gaze up,
beyond the galaxies, more and more
my eyes become only light,
two more burning nebula standing sentinel
against and about and around all comers.

the cold is our communion,
night the telescope through which
we each find only evidence of the other,
divided by space folding ever again
in on itself, and yet unyielding witness
to our mutual and constant comradeship.

Midnight Walk

Madness must be kept at bay –
I suppose – but what is madness,
but a lifting of this filmy lens
that keeps you from my vision?

If I strain, I can see you still:
Even now, one shadow rises behind another,
a wind moves trees that make no sound,
night comes apace but darkness malingers.

Shall I pretend, then, you are not there? Shall I cling
        to this vaunted sanity
and turn away from you?
Perhaps those who talk to ghosts
are the only ones who see the real.
Hush now, the trees are talking,
I must copy down their words.

a miner's task

I watch the dark as she chisels
out the stars, and I think how long
and thankless is her work – we fickle mortals,
who hang on light as spiders must dangle
from their silks, imagine she is our enemy,
when hers alone is the patient and weary hand
that lifts the hammer again and again,
driving herself deeper into the night
till prism'd splendor pours unbroken out.

find another lover

the sun is a stalker

lurking menace whose fiery glare strips
artifice and edifice and leaves me stark
and bare – I hate the fiend,
loathe his hot breath on the back of my neck,
dread the burning caress that exhilarates
when I would vegetate, that prompts, provokes,
prevails on me to look, look, see,
when I would bide in darkness
and wait on dreams – damned demigod
who fancies himself a lover unparalleled,
imagining every green leaf unfurling at his touch
a precious supplicant – perhaps the glut
is even right, but I hate him still,
hate how he hovers, barely out of sight,
as midnight struggles to take
the summer sky, only to lurch out again,
great golden galoot, and gleefully shout
his bold halloos. Let him stalk then.
Let him smolder and couch,
let him linger and sigh and cast about dramatically
for every watching eye. It will not be mine.
I will be away, I will burrow
and sleep, I will hibernate till winter.

wildfire season

smoke and ash and fireweed cotton dance
macabrely in the falling sunlight, shaft
after shaft of relentless light poured unchecked
onto a parched earth: summer is tired,
gasping for air, her skirts faded and torn,
but her partner will not let her go,
swinging her again and again across
 a matted floor beaten hard and dry
by their pounding steps – I feel her heart
beating in the sullen air, frantic, arrhythmic,
like the wings of a honeybee
caught between the screen and the glass.
she would go, give leave to her sister autumn
to take a turn upon the floor,
but her partner's grip is iron, his smile oil.
we will dance until the winter then,
and see what rest but death we find.

beyond the tent

perhaps it will not be so hard
as I imagine: already the grass here
feels artificial beneath my feet,
the light more fluorescent than moonlit,
and these words that no longer fit my tongue
perhaps were not my words at all:

maybe it will be like going home,
catching hold of starlight strand by strand
and divesting my flesh of all its clay –
already I feel it shifting with in me,
this awkward soul weary of its ill-fitting cloth.

I only need know that when my trapeze catches,
on the other side of the net,
that you will seize my hand and hold it fast.

the mutations of grief

the weight of hope

I found your rooms were as ordered
as the hole in your head: quiet, still, unsubtle chaos,
all the hope gone grey and ill-defined,
indistinct amid all the other mess
you must have tried but finally despaired
of settling onto any shelf strong enough
to bear up under its growing weight.

It's not fear, after all, that gets unmanageable.
Fear keeps generally to the regular route:
it likes coursing veins and pounding hearts
and trembling breaths. It even paces out
its advance and sweeps the floor in its retreat.
No, hope is the ungovernable one,
its unwieldy shape ever shifting in the arms,
growing heavier and heavier day by day,
adding to its weight till every muscle strains
and the lungs burn to keep from dropping it.

From dropping it – oh, the mess it made
when it slipped from your hands
and landed here, in all the rubble and details
they said you had to sort to make a life.
Receipts and regulations and return envelopes –
the cellophane rattles in my hand,
but there is no missive I can read,
no sense to make of all this mangled alphabet,
no return from here.

there must be an outside

despair for a bird must be an aviary:
a cage, after all, is its own hope,
its finite bounds and unapologetic bars
proof of what waits beyond,
as the walls of a cell stand testament
to the open air and open earth outside –
there must always be an outside

but in the aviary, the bird may fly,
may travel tree to tree, limb to limb,
reach the sky, taste the earth,
but still, and always, there is no out,
and every flight finds the same end.

you could not make out the walls, I know.
you searched and searched for the bars,
for the lock, for any sign that this existence
was only a prison and not the whole,
and finding no bound, you drew your own
in this red line
and crossed it.

the approach

I breathe you in like smoke.
your ashes fill my veins
and turn my blood to sludge:
I thought to live with you,
but now you live in me,
and I am evicted, evacuated
from all my rooms: smoke and ash
are all my breath, my being,
and I am lost in the grey.

I thought to carry you all,
but the ground is soft, so soft,
and the moss so thick,
and step by step I was swallowed.
It is all so grey, so awful grey.

let me eat the blame

what is tumor, and what is tissue?
this is the wrong question: I must love
what I have tamed, I must tame
what I have borne, and then I must
make it somehow feral and free again.

I will not begrudge the eaters their meal
or the grave its prey, I will not hate bread
because it has killed the yeast.
I honed a blade that swung unready,
but still I love the bloody edge:
it is not the fault of teeth to bite
or claws that furrows drive.

it lies in all of life to die, and this of all
makes us the envy of immortals,
for so we live much more than they.
but ah, the bite of gold against the teeth.
however precious, how it hurts,
it hurts.

more than metaphor

how can something that is not cold
feel cold, when cold is nothing more
than the sensation of its being?
how can you in every aspect appear absent,
when absence necessarily does not appear
at all? – and still, your outline gapes in void,
your movement through the air creates
only an acknowledgement of where ripples
ought to be, and where your hand
touches mine, where by definition heat
meets heat, this phantom cold is all I feel.

unwanted spring

loss is life as much as its end:
we never grieve so bitterly
as in that moment we realize,
that for an hour, or more,
we did not grieve at all.
the absence of absence makes the belly ache,
and when the crocus blooms,
we weep – how furiously we weep –
for frost that no longer falls.

totem

I have rejected this place.
I have refused her,
and she will not get in,
however long she knocks.
from the first, she made love to me,
sweet and soft, with her cold voice
and colder hands and eyes full of mysteries,
but hers is the body of my despair,
in her belly rots my beloved,
on her shoulders sit the ravens
who have swallowed his eyes,
and I cannot forgive.
I stand on her feet,
and she holds me fast,
but I will not let her in.

Mt. Redoubt, Minor Eruption

chaos silently unfurls, silhouetted by sunset,
the mad fury of earth bidding tribute
to the passage of the star – of my star, too,
fires all burned out, who sleeps curled
in still more silent slumber beneath loam
and peat and fern – the mountain, after all,
is not truly silent, merely far away
(you too are far, too far to hear my voice)
and yet the quiet of the drama
as the plume exuberates from earth to sky
appeals to me: I picture exploding rock,
tumbling dirt, steam and fire and ash,
all voicelessly proceeding in reckless choreograph:

I cannot imitate that grace
lent by hours and miles of sea –
I am raw and awkward and much too loud,
my grief banging and reverberating
from tree to tree, ill-fit to any rock or leaf:
I do not fit on the earth,
and you (and he, and she, and they)
are locked beneath it, and all my will
is in that ash, revolting shameless against this floor
of heaven gated against us, till it is swallowed,
swallowed, suffocated by the sea.

hard-packed earth

I am arroyo,
dry, empty, cracked, and still

but when your rains fell,
I became torrent, became flood

my voice a shout
that for an hour or two

drowned out even the thunder:
I carried you

where you could not have gone alone.
Now I am dry again,

but I cannot be channel
if I am fluid as sand.

I am arroyo, not river,
but still I know the deluge.

it is not real

only a glass divides me
from the night as it approaches,
peering warily 'round the tree trunks
and creeping through the dandelions,
still – it is not real.

my eyes make it seem real as they darken,
the clock insists the time has come,
the time has passed,
but still I sit in a pool of light,
blanketed against the encroaching chill,
and I insist –
it is not real.

I felt your cooling skin,
I watched the sheet not rise, not rise,
and not rise still with any breath.
I said good-bye, and still –
it is not real.

I sit in a pool of light.
Perhaps it is I who am not real.

lies wrapped in sheets

you look like a man, like a stranger,
formal and stiff and held together,
and I don't like it.
you looked like a boy when I saw you last –
or at least, like the space
where a boy had been,
clammy and pale, slack-faced,
with a tube in your mouth, lips swollen
and eyelids stretched too tightly over your eyes,
your hair still damp with those last,
too-hard endeavors – more yourself
than this serene-faced obelisk dressed
in your clothes. I miss that boy
and all the hope bound tight in all his sins,
I miss the luxury of rage and fear
that might have yet turned to trust,
I miss the maybes and the almosts
and the next times. I will trace out
this space that held a boy
and let go this scarecrow, leave him
to frighten the death-eaters away.
I am not afraid of boys, though sometimes
they are afraid of the dark,
and I am heavy with night:
still, perhaps from the voodoo dolls we made
of each other, we will become talismans
after all, you who need no guide anywhere
but an anchor to yesterday,
and me who has always been lost.

shift into me

I am watching rock become sand –
what ought to have taken decades,
what some escape entirely,
has fallen on you in an instant,
and you are sloughed away, dissolved,
undone, all your solid become liquid,
become air: but you have only changed state.
what once I held in my hand,
I will drink into my belly,
I will breathe into my lungs,
I will make of you all my bones
and walk when you cannot
until you change state again.
who knows what will become of us,
of you, of me?
who cares, either – sand or stone,
you are all my grit,
foundation, whet, and polish.

surrogate

I hold onto the wooden man
you've left to keep your place,
a soul-anchor, a voodoo doll,
marionette with a familiar face
whose jerks and stops and flourishes
pretend at grief but stand so distant
from the howling keen I can just hear,
if I stand very still,
if I clutch very tightly this cold, smooth wood –

you are lost in the other-world,
in the shadowscape where still the shade
you seek eludes you. this wooden man
rocks and weeps, he looks like you
and again like a stranger, but I will keep him
safely on his peg till you find your way
out of the between. this wooden man
and I, we hold your place.

keep to the path, love,
don't venture past the trees.

paper-cranes

his fingers folded the moon like origami –
light peeped between his fingers,
spilled on the ground, but he let it lie:

I watched him, rapt, lulled
to stillness by the deftness of his fingers,
and when fold after fold tucked
the silver foil away till only black remained,
still I stared, light-blind, at the darkness
where last I'd seen him stand.

I became accustomed to absence in the end,
no longer straining after what was lost,
but curling into my own aching circle,
I found moon-scraps still glowing,
stuck to the soles of my feet.

former shades

the dead have no cause to lie,
so why does this ghost haunt me
with all your promises unkept? –

ah, you are not dead,
but still a ghost, a spectre of yourself,
bound up in lies you tell
your present and all the truths
you told – you tell – our past.

do not fret, my love.
no need to tread the boards,
rattle the shutters, whisper on the wind.
I know the whole.

rest easy. I will keep your oaths
my secret, keep your keeping them
more secret still.
we go on.

supplicant

sometimes the sacred space you think
you seek is not sunshine and birdsong and the voice of
     the river:
sometimes what is sacred stinks of vomit
and blood and not nearly enough fear,
sometimes it sounds less like the sea and more like,
don't let him aspirate, turn his head,
is he still breathing,
sometimes you don't know you are in the Holy of Holies
till all the holy is gone,
the agony is gone,
the breathing is gone,
and you are all alone with your dirty bare feet.

eavesdropping at tables and trailheads

the old man and the ice

fissured and worn like the face
of an old man, the glacier sounds
like an old man, too, creaking
and groaning before lapsing
into a long, still silence:

the unwary, the unschooled, might imagine
that the power and force of the earth
rests in the rumble and the roar of the river
that tumbles across the glacier's feet,
but the treachery of the ancients abides
in patience and in cunning: here plunge crevasses,
here howl calves, here lure frozen fields,
and when the warning sounds,
when an old man's groan becomes the crow
of ageless triumph, it will be too late

for escape: but a splinter falls, a shard,
and the river cows in terror before the calf,
the man shrinks before his mortality,
the glacier itself bows before divisibility.
We are all reduced, but we are not all mighty.

who needs angst when we have snapchat?

they discuss it over coffee cups
and cell phones, consequent with
the color of the sky and the casual scorn
of their coworkers – which would be
more fun? should I slit my wrists
or jump off a cliff or just accept
the cliché of the overdose?

I'd like to imagine their flippancy
a defense, a means of rendering powerless
what might terrify, but they've already
rambled on to locker contents and sleeping partners,
oblivious to the weight of the words
they've left lying there in the café
between us: how should I kill myself?

what color should I dye my eyebrows?
who will find me?
how short should I cut my hair?
would it be easier for my mom
if I used a gun or if I used a knife?
these cupcakes are making me fat.

rain on the boards

the paper dolls of politics don't long persist
in the climate here: the rain is too constant,
the wind unconcerned for the fate
of yard-signs and bumper stickers and leaflets,
the galloping fungi and ferns that devour
every dead thing long before it decays
are unlikely to leave the fat carcasses
of buyers and feeders and fakers untouched:

no boots touch the ground or the ship-decks
here without cameras and waiting cars as witness,
grassroots are for city folks who imagine
their cultivated lawns and measured clippings amount
to resistance and rebellion even as rhetoric reduces
itself to single-word epithets – nothing is more desperate
now than it has ever been, but we summon invaders
and oppressors to justify flags and banners,
pitch our battles with carefully negotiated outcomes,
glorious defeats and graceful victories: pageantry
is become its own purpose in a play
with no supporting actors, no subplots,
and we blind to the villain in us all.

Murders in Embassies

The spatter is a distraction:
as expected, we chase every drop of blood,
trace outlines in chalk, follow the path
of projectiles to their origins and posit plotlines,
but the spatter is the distraction.

Contrary to the musings of the dressers
and dissectors of the dead, the body is no book,
and this is all its worth to tyrants –
whatever story is written in indignity and gore
is told to obscure, to blot out, to silence
the story still held behind stitched lips.

So don shawls for the dead, if you must,
don robes to judge and condemn the knife,
but when the room is clean
and the dead are buried, the story will remain untold.
The spatter is a distraction.

school lunches

it's the most important thing, the napkin:
quietly she lines up the elements of lunch
on the cafeteria table, praying for invisibility,
wishing for comrades, conscious of the scorn
that any notice might provoke

or might not

it's the anticipation that sours her stomach,
the smells of white bread and deodorant turning sound
into color as a kaleidoscope of voices rushes
over her – she clings to the napkin,
hopes not to see her name bursting behind her eyes
in purple and black and green

but the flavor of bologna is not the flavor of hope,
and no willful chewing can ease these belly pains
or stop the words graffiti-ing over her hunched back –
fat, ugly, four-eyes, nerd, stupid, pathetic –
she tears the napkin into tiny, precise pieces,
knowing that no soap and water, no cloth,
can scrub these colors off her skin.

coffeeshop scarecrow

all the corners are taken:
window glass and open floor lay bare
the bones of my unease, but the corners
against which I must bolster my defenses
neither fly nor walk; still, I crave
a frame which might pretend support,
an angle at which to prop a line,
however imprecise its points:

I draw the scarecrow, braid its hair,
set it at a table with a cup at one hand
and a pencil at the other, but beneath
the cotton and the straw, the weevils eat,
hollowing out every diagram on which
I hang my parts of speech.

three dollars a nose

they'd managed to kill hundreds,
he tells me, but had to wait for the tide
to go out and leave stranded
the heavy bodies of the pregnant seals –
no time to skin them all, but no need:
they ran out with knives and raced the sea,
slicing and gathering as fast as they could –
three dollars a nose, he explains.
damn government, mismanages everything.
he shifts his heft in his seat
and changes topics, mournfully recounting
how a lynx had eaten the young sandhill crane
that had been visiting his yard.
juxtaposition makes my head hurt,
and I am glad not to belong.

reunion

woodsmoke adrift on frosty air:
filigree leaves sigh and settle
on the forest floor, their little huffs
puffing against my ankles, insistent
I acknowledge their company,
though I am all but heedless
of their tiny rages – I am listening
to my brother's voice, and he tells
me stories of all I have forgot,
his discordant cadence the familiar jangle
of peace that makes melody of discord,
channel of rapids, path of stone:
I reach the river at last,
plunge hands and ankles into his icy depths,
and remember my name
when he speaks it.

river of ice

the river waits

holds itself in abeyance,
dreaming of old seas and a younger sun,
submitting in silence to a yoke of stone
till its burden can be laid
in the arms of the ocean:

man, brief walker, mourns the journey,
but the ice is wiser than he,
the ice remembers and the ice hopes

was river, is river still, will river be,
and earth, stone, bone, or flesh,
all will be shaped by its currents.

the river waits.
the river hopes.

tea with god

semi:

You are starlight trapped
in a stone, a jellyfish trembling
out its last pulse on black sand
beneath a full moon. Beam.
Pulse. Beat. Break.
Crack open the stone.
Split the shore and bring in the sea,
pound against my palm.
Shake out this end and promise a beginning.

lost between thumb and forefinger

so the butterfly, they say, becomes the current
and the coyote becomes the buffalo
and in the end, we all become the stars:
but I am a devotee of the insignificant,
a student and adorer of all that is small and singular,
and I find no peace in subsumation.

let me worship the hollow of your pelvic bone,
let me map the lines beside your eyes,
and make histories of all your petty follies;
if deification is promised to the absorbed and the consumed,
then leave me poor and mortal among the snails
and the dandelions – we are brief,
but we are we, and I am I,
and you all my delight.
I am a devotee of the insignificant.

strange classroom

the power of the talon rests
in purpose: here there is no strength
for the sake of strength, no grace in artifice –
heavy with the weight of the eagle,
sharpened oft on shell and bone,
the talons seize the fish and hold him fast
while the steady, ruthless beak tears
flesh from skin and scale: I sit,
silent student at this indifferent teacher's feet,
and learn of hunger and satiation,
of predation without pretense.

I listen to my own breath, finding rhythm
in the waves, and count the pulses
of my heart as if I knew their sum.

I do not know their sum.
I am the fish, I am the eagle,
I am the jelly, shimmering on the sand.

other

there is a child who cannot be comforted
but seeks solace
who cannot be held but cannot let go
who builds worlds of words
but is marooned on an island whose sand
did not come from this sea

there is an alone no love can alter.

first he named the animals

It is not only the coward
who dies a thousand deaths:
what other task has the writer
than to bear in her body
the thousand deaths of man,
to take into her veins every poison,
to bare her flesh to every blade and thorn,
to break her bones beneath the weight
of every grief, all rancor, all villainy:

monsters and myths, all things discarded,
the common and the oblique – all have a form
consummate with grace once their edges
have been traced out with the words,
the only words, the precise and particular words,
and to this purpose she bends all her being,
to augur out the frame of pain,
and in the naming of all things,
to find a moniker her own.

traveling companions

I wonder where I've been

when your eyes meet mine
in the steam of black coffee on an icy morning,
or when you propel me forward,
broad hand in the small of my back,
through a crowd where you've never stood

I wonder 'round what corners
I've turned just before you,
in what strange beds you last saw
my face before falling asleep

I wonder where I've been.

trader

it is a false and wicked alchemy
but I am the meanest addict
to its fools' gold: I fill my pockets,
stuff my drawers, hoard the stuff,
poison in its false promises,
and insist it will offer fair exchange
in this market of breaths and hours:

like all markets, this one exists
only on a point of agreement,
and all its traders, buyers, and sellers
are junkies like me – we line up words
on ticker tape, and lacking discipline,
buy high and sell low,
insistent that this currency of cruelty
and trash we have stamped in gleaming alloy
be honored for its intent rather than its worth.

only the altered are deceived,
but we are all altered:
we watch the towers crumble and imagine
that story will resurrect the struts,
that we have only to assign a name
to animate the soul in the construct.

Cuppa

I watch her fingers wrap reflexively
around the mug, watch her draw scented steam
into her lungs like an intoxicant,
and I wonder, what does God do
instead of drinking tea?

It's a strange enough impulse of ours:
on meeting the inexplicable, the unacceptable,
the unbearable, to turn for solace
to comforts most fleeting, most ephemeral,
as if somehow hot liquid briefly meeting
spasmed, aching flesh could somehow touch
this chasm'd grief into which every thought
slides, mudbound cliffs crumbling into an empty sea –

futilely we stroke the feral cats
of our souls and wish it were consolation
instead of trespass – and I wonder,
what beggar'd effort does God attempt,
what wild angels shrug away
his awkward caress, and does he ever long
for a taste of tea, for some insipid promise
that all will be well,
that things won't look so bad in the morning.

acknowledgements

"Spendthrift" was published February 2019 in the *Folio World Tree* Issue.

"A miner's task" was published Spring 2019 by the *Brushfire Literature & Arts Journal*.

Other Titles from Otis Books

Aldo Palazzeschi, *The Arsonist*

Dennis Phillips, *Navigation: Selected Poems, 1985–2010*

Antonio Porta, *Piercing the Page: Selected Poems 1958–1989*

Eric Priestley, *For Keeps*

Sophie Rachmuhl, *A Higher Form of Politics:*
       The Rise of a Poetry Scene, Los Angeles, 1950–1990

Dorothy Rice, *Gray Is the New Black*

Norberto Luis Romero, *The Obscure Side of the Night*

Olivia Rosenthal, *We're Not Here to Disappear*

Noah Ross, *Swell*

Amelia Rosselli, *Hospital Series*

———, *War Variations*

All of our titles are available from Small Press Distribution.
Order them at www.spdbooks.org